Harriet Adams Sawyer

Souvenir of Asheville N.C., or the Skyland

Harriet Adams Sawyer

Souvenir of Asheville N.C., or the Skyland

ISBN/EAN: 9783337036379

Printed in Europe, USA, Canada, Australia, Japan

Cover: Foto ©Andreas Hilbeck / pixelio.de

More available books at **www.hansebooks.com**

Souvenir
of

ASHEVILLE,

OR THE

SKY-LAND.

BY

MRS HARRIET ADAMS SAWYER.

ST. LOUIS:
NIXON-JONES PRINTING CO.
1892.

All Rights Reserved.
Mrs. Harriet Adams Sawyer.
1892.

CONTENTS.

	Page.
Asheville, or Sky Land — Situation,	9
Asheville in Brief,	14
Resources,	21
Flowers,	27

ASHEVILLE PLATEAU.
- Nature of Climate,
- Temperature,
- Humidity,
- Wind, ... 33–41
- Atmospheric Pressure,
- Rainfall,
- Sunshine and Cloudiness,

Merits of Climate,	42
The Brave's Farewell, Poem,	49
Hotels, Kenilworth Inn,	57
Battery Park,	65
Hotel Belmont,	73
Oakland Heights,	81
Schools, Ravenscroft High School,	85
Asheville Female College,	86
Bingham School,	86

PLACES OF INTEREST TO VISITORS:
- Mt. Mitchell,
- Grave of Rev. Elisha Mitchell, D.D., Poem,
- Richmond Hill,
- Pearson's Bridge,
- Connolly's Ford,
- Old Cabin Home,
- Esmerelda's Cabin, ... 91–103
- Lover's Leap,
- Mt. Pisgah,
- Reem's Creek Falls,
- Cæsar's Head,
- Round Knob,
- Paint Rock,
- Chimney Rocks,

Places and Distances, etc,	103
Time Table,	104

ILLUSTRATIONS.

Asheville from Town Mountain.
The Square.
Bank.
City Hall.
Baptist Church.
Above the Clouds.
Mt. Mitchell.
Tilling the Soil.
French Broad, from Richmond Hill.
Old Cabin Home.
Connolly's Ford
Paint Rock.
A Shady Nook.
Cæsar's Head.
Pisgah, from Battery Park.
Blondon Donkey.
Boating on Swannanoa.
Lover's Leap.
Bailey's Bend on French Broad.
On French Broad near Hot Springs.
Pearson's Bridge.
Reem's Creek Falls.
The Sluice, on French Broad.
Hotel and Fountain at Round Knob.
Ravenscroft School.
Kenilworth Inn.
Battery Park.
Belmont.
Oakland Heights.

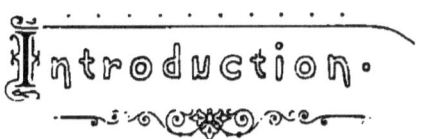

Introduction.

So many and great are the attractions and advantages offered by this modern Arcadia, it would be impossible to set them forth within the scope designed for this little souvenir. Accordingly, we shall only present, in so brief a form that ''he who runs may read,'' a few of the salient points which make Asheville pre-eminently desirable as a place of resort, either for health, or pleasure, in Summer or Winter. Our illustrations will show something of the picturesqueness of Asheville and its environment, with its principal hotels and public buildings. We are confident that those who catch a glimpse through this vista, of its charms, will be impelled to investigate in person the larger claims of this Sky-Land to popular favor and patronage.

ASHEVILLE, OR SKY-LAND.

Beautiful for Situation.

IN THIS little souvenir of ASHEVILLE, it is our purpose to let it, so far as is possible, speak for itself. It has been said, "Figures do not lie." Is not this statement equally true of photography? Claiming that it is so, we give you, on a very small scale, a peep into this "SKY-LAND."

As "*multum in parvo*" is our motto, it has been exceedingly difficult to select from the hundreds of views, presented by the photographer, the small number which we can insert. The more we scanned the varied charms depicted, the more serious became the difficulty; but, at last we have selected a few, which must be received by the reader as typical only, of the indescribable and unlimited expanse of grandeur and beauty, which Nature has so lavishly spread before us in this land of the sky.

"Lift thine eyes, O, lift thine eyes unto the mountains, from whence cometh thine help."

To the ever-moving population of our country, especially to those who are seekers after health, and, not less truly to those who need only seek after the delights of travel, comes the question yearly — "Where shall we go?" Many places in the country answer the query most satisfactorily if you only wish a transient abode.

To the North we are pointed for cooling breezes in summer, and to the South for balmy air and invigorating sunshine in winter, but alas! between these two sections, there lies a vast area of territory, to compass which, one must expend a deal of strength, time and money.

So, Nature, our kind mother, always so ready to minister to her children in life, and to gently cover and shelter them in death,—has prepared this "Sky-Land," this city of refuge alike from the blizzards of the northern winters, and the sultry southern summer's sun, where her children may hold high carnival, where the winters are softened, and where the summers are fanned by breezes fresh from the mountains, and where the weary may rest in an all the year jubilee.

What is there to delight the eye, or to inspire the poet's dream, that is not found in Asheville and vicinity? High mountains — dewy vales — sloping highlands, — rivers vying with any sung by poet, or painted by artist, whose very names breathe of music and song. "French Broad" "Swannanoa."

Can you not almost hear the splashing of the oar and see the canoe of the red man, with its gaily bedecked occupant, summoning all his bravery and muscular force, to guide it o'er those darkling, turbulent waters of the French Broad, singing the while his wild song, as, on either hand, some dashing torrent, falling from its high source in some adjacent mountain, adds its deep chorus to his melody? Then, with the red man's ever ready sympathy with Nature, and her moods, as he passes along to the more peaceful waters of the Swannanoa, his voice falls, and his wild war song is changed to one of mournful tenderness as he sings now of the "Great Spirit," and of the "Happy Hunting Grounds."

Here are the forests primeval. But, as youth ever loves to adorn and enliven age, behold the many vines whose cling-

BOATING ON THE SWANNANOA.

ing tendrils climb to the highest branches, and cover the time-marked trunks of these mountain patriarchs.

On these shores how the ferns love to grow and flowers to bloom, decking shore and mountain side in every hue. How the birds sing! And still the deer darts in and out, among the giants of the forest and the vine-trellised hills, finding alternate sun and shade.

Who shall attempt to describe a sunset in this "Sky-Land?" Surely you will gaze enraptured, and seem to hear sky-voices, which sound as if not far away, saying:

"Lift up your heads, O ye gates! even lift them up ye everlasting doors, and the King of Glory shall come in. Who is this King of Glory? The Lord of Hosts. He is the King of Glory."

Would you get near to Nature's heart? Hither come. With canopy of bluest blue, with sunlight, now flashing gems of every color over all, and anon, such shadows! As the sun sinks, giant forms of darkness stalk over the valley, the birds hide, the flowers close their petals, and stillness audible prevails.

ASHEVILLE IN BRIEF.

IN 1812, Asheville, an old and picturesquely located mountain city, was simply a trading-post. In 1833 the place was incorporated and for years was known as Morristown. This name gave place later to that of Asheville, in honor of Samuel Ashe, of New Hanover. Its growth has been phenomenal. While it stands pre-eminent as a resort for health and pleasure, in both summer and winter, it deserves high rank as a city of great business resources and importance. Upon these we shall in this place dwell very briefly. There are 16 manufacturing and lumber establishments within the city limits, with an aggregate capital of $800,000, doing an annual business of $1,100,000. Real estate transactions are very extensive.

The inducements to visitors and residents are all that could be desired. The best of educational advantages are offered. There are sixteen churches representing all denominations. In Asheville, the Sabbath is honored, the people attend church and a sensation of restfulness may be enjoyed which is not often found at so popular a resort. Some of the finest hotels in America are here. Those most popular are, Kenilworth Inn, Battery Park, Hotel Belmont, Oakland Heights, Swannanoa, Grand Central, Oaks, and Glen Rock. To those wishing less expensive accommodations, are offered many fine boarding houses — among which Mr. McCapes takes high rank. There are also facilities offered at reasonable rates for light housekeeping.

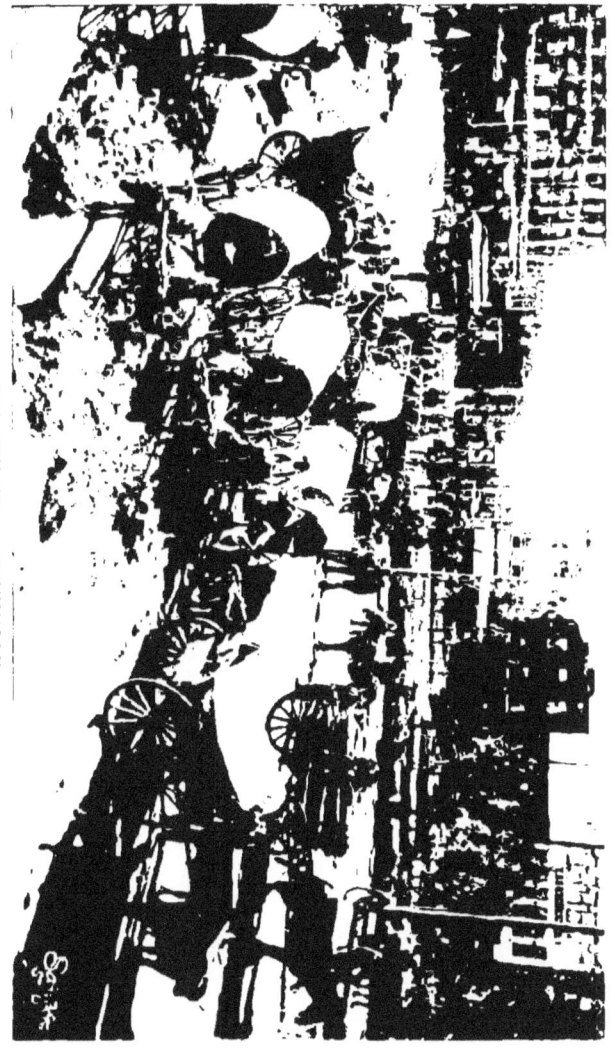

THE SQUARE, ASHEVILLE.

The markets are always well supplied with all of the best things which the seasons bring, and at low prices. Large appropriations have been recently made for street improvements, which are rapidly progressing. Those particularly fond of mosquitoes must look elsewhere for a habitation, as this very musical and social, although not altogether popular element is not found in Asheville. In brief Asheville

Has a Telephone Exchange.
It has a progressive Y. M. C. A.
It has a good system of sewerage.
It has an efficient Fire Department.
It has a well-drilled military company.
It has an altitude of nearly 2,300 feet.
It has the Gamewell Fire Alarm System.
It has a public Library and Reading Room.
It has a progressive Mayor and City Council.
It has four railroads running in all directions.
It has three banks and two more in prospect.
It has the handsomest Opera House in the State.
It has a score of eminent and skillful physicians.
It has a large number of first-class livery stables.
It has excellent schools, both public and private.
It has two large and well-equipped Sanitariums.
It has two electric light companies and a gas company.
It has energetic, progressive and wide-awake merchants.
It has two daily and half a dozen weekly newspapers.
It has a population of 12,000 and about 100,000 visitors yearly.
It has dry, bracing air, and a delightful climate all of the year.
It has a well conducted hospital with an efficient medical corps.

It has an electric street railway traversing all parts of the city.

It has a good system of water works, giving an ample supply of pure water.

It has a new Government Post-Office in course of construction and a new City Hall.

It has flourishing Masonic, Knights of Pythias, Odd Fellows, Knights of Honor, Sons of Temperance lodges, besides several labor organizations.

It had an ice factory, cotton mill, two shoe factories, furniture factory, cigar factory, numerous wood working factories, tobacco factories, flour mills, broom factory, etc.

Mr. Vanderbilt's Mansion.

Mr. Geo. W. Vanderbilt, the great millionaire, has selected Asheville in which to locate and develop what promises to be the grandest of American homes. " Vanderbilt Park " is composed of 8,000 acres of most charming variety and beauty, lying between the Swannanoa and French Broad rivers. Upon the summit of this vast area is being constructed the Vanderbilt mansion. Its erection will require years of time and millions of money. The grand approach to the residence is through an avenue two miles and a half in length. Mr. Vanderbilt is doing the work through his agent, Mr. McNamee, and only makes occasional visits to note its progress. There is a force employed of 300 hands, and 50 teams. Plans are being developed for costly residences, outbuildings, farm houses, stables, etc., besides the laying out of extensive drives, and roads; planting of orchards and forming of plantations of evergreens, or other trees. This surely is indicative of the popularity, and progress of Asheville. Other gentlemen of New York and Philadelphia are also building splendid homes here.

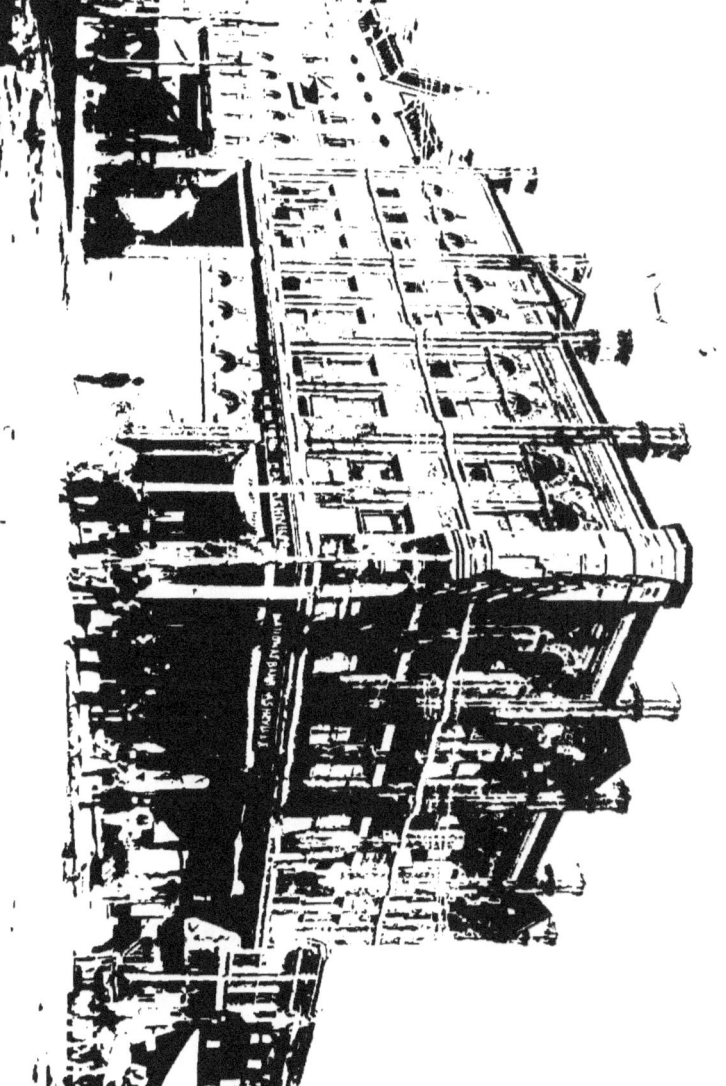

NATIONAL BANK OF ASHEVILLE.

RESOURCES.

From "Lindsey's Guide Book" I quote the following:

WESTERN North Carolina is not only exceedingly fertile but abounds in the richer minerals, and needs but the magic wand of the capitalist waved over it to become one of the richest sections of this Union. Occupying one-third of the entire area of the State, and possessing more than a quarter of a million of inhabitants, its present prospects are by no means disagreeable; but its prominent citizens, of all walks of life, are anxious for immigration and development of the rich stores of gold, iron, copper, mica, etc., now buried in the hills. Let no one fancy that this mountain region is undesirable as an agricultural country; there are few richer and better adapted to European emigration. The staple productions are tobacco, corn, wheat, rye, oats and hay; all vegetables grow abundantly, and the whole country is admirably fitted for grazing. The level bottom lands are under fine cultivation; the uplands and slopes produce rich wheat; the ash, the sugar maple, the hickory and the oak are abundant; the white pine is rafted down the Pigeon river in large quantities yearly. But the exceptional fertility of most of the ranges throughout all the counties is the great pride of the section. The sides and tops of the mountains are in many cases covered with a thick vegetable mold, in which grow flourishing trees and rank grasses. Five thousand feet above the sea level one finds grasses and weeds that remind him of the lower swamp region. Cattle are kept in excellent condition all winter on the "evergreen" growing along the sides of the higher chains. Winter and summer, before the ravages of war thinned out their stock, the farmers kept hundreds of cattle on the mountains, feeding entirely on grass.

The valleys of the French Broad and Swannanoa offer for all kinds of husbandry an inviting field, while the climatic conditions are more than favorable. Agriculture is one of the interests tributary to Asheville, while the forest growth is a subject now attracting the attention of capitalists. In the country contiguous to the place there are to be found the yellow pine, oak of almost every variety, black walnut, chestnut, locust, poplar, black birch, cherry, maple, sycamore, mulberry, sassafras, dogwood, and other well-known varieties of native woods.

Nearly 160 minerals, simple and compound, are found in Western North Carolina, many of them being extremely rare and of great value. In the French Broad valley gold exists in many localities, while future explorations will no doubt lead to other discoveries. This country possesses literally mountains of wealth in mica, this section supplying nearly one-half the demand throughout the world."

Fruit Growing.

"As a fruit growing section Western North Carolina enjoys peculiar advantages. Apples, peaches, pears and apricots thrive well, and find a congenial home among these mountains. As for apples there is probably no part of the country where they flourish so well as in this section.

The Centennial medal at Philadelphia, awarded for fine apples, was taken by Capt. Natt. Atkinson, of this place, who was engaged in fruit growing at that time, near Asheville; and in the following year at the American Pomological Society's meeting, in the city of Baltimore, the same gentleman was awarded the Wilder medal for one hundred varieties of finest apples."

TILLING THE SOIL.

PAINT ROCK.

Wills Bros., Architects, Asheville.

FIRST BAPTIST CHURCH.

Flowers.

IN WINTER the visitor finds the holly trees in their beautiful symmetry, laden with bright red berries, and the poetic mistletoe, hanging in long masses from the limbs of the trees, and while the mountains are still snow-capped, the dainty violet will greet the traveler's feet. The hawthorne also abounds in December. In the spring the wild rhododendron, that royally luxuriant flower in pink and white, fringes every stream with beauty. With it comes the graceful azalia, laden with red or yellow lily-shaped blossoms, and the pink clusters of ivy massed in their setting of green. The kalmia follows. In June and July the heather and houstonias abound. Then those sweet visitants, so impartial in their favors to this broad land of ours, the forget-me-not and lily-of-the-valley, seem to do their utmost and best for the "Sky-Land." Being a native of Maine, how happy was I, one day, in mid-winter, to find upon the mountain side, the trailing arbutus, so dear to the heart of every New Englander.

> O trailing arbutus, you beautiful thing,
> How many and sweet are the memories ye bring
> To the child of New England! When far from his home,
> In the land of the stranger, your picture will come.
> And carry him back, in the twilight's soft hour,
> Over prairie and mountain with magical power,—
> And the long-banished pilgrim far off in the west
> Again is a child, with your bloom on his breast.

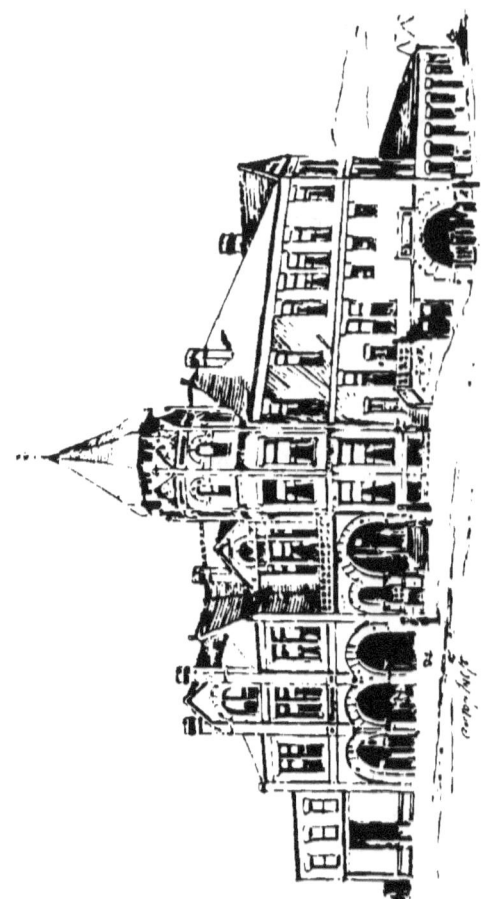

Wills Bros., Architects, Asheville.

CITY HALL.

OLD CABIN HOME.

ABOVE THE CLOUDS.

ASHEVILLE PLATEAU.

From a paper read before the County Medical Society, at Asheville, January 2d, 1888, by Samuel Westray Battle, M. D., P. A. Surgeon U. S. Navy, Asheville, N. C., proprietor Battery Park Hotel: having his generous permission to do so, I quote extensively, knowing that his authority is unquestionably reliable:

THE Asheville or the Appalachian plateau with Asheville in its middle, is an elevated tableland somewhat triangular in shape, embracing some six thousand square miles of western North Carolina, with a general elevation of two thousand feet above the sea level, though there are points from one thousand to fifteen hundred feet higher to the northward of Asheville.

"It is upward of a hundred and fifty miles long with an average width of twenty-five miles. It lies west of the Blue Ridge and east of the Great Smoky Mountains, its surface being much cut up by cross-chains and spurs of its eastern and western barriers, as the Black Mountain from the Blue Ridge, the Balsam, the Cullowee and Nantahala from the Smokies. Hills, valleys, rivers and forests, so diversify this intra montane expanse as to make it lovely and restful to the eye beyond the power of my pen to portray.

"The great Appalachian chain, upon reaching North Carolina, stands sponsor to a section which should be, and I predict will be, the great sanitorium of our eastern country. As if conscious of its future importance it has seen fit to guard the plateau with its loftiest and grandest peaks, a half hundred of which tower to a height upward of six thousand feet, and a dozen pierce the sky at an altitude greater than that of Mount Washington, or any point east of the Rocky Mountains. As far as scenery goes, 'age cannot wither, nor custom stale its infinite variety' — a point too little thought of in casting about for a suitable climate.

"Asheville, the county seat of Buncombe, well situated 250 feet above the waters of the French Broad and Swannanoa rivers, and one mile from their confluence, is itself 2,350 feet above tide water. The entire region is covered with a luxuriant growth of primitive forest of pine, balsam and the handsomest of the deciduous variety of trees generally, the mountains being wooded to their very summits, an unusual and an attractive feature which delights the eye and at once impresses most favorably the tourist and health seeker. The scenic effects to be had here are a proper food for the eye of the sick and the well, and in rounding up the complement of a health resort are not to be lost sight of. The Blue Ridge to the eastward is the water shed of the mountain region of Western North Carolina, the plateau being well watered by clear mountain streams the general direction of which is westward toward the Mississippi.

Nature of Climate.

THE climate of the Asheville Plateau may be called a medium altitude, dry, all-the-year-round climate, enjoying peculiar advantages and many attractive features by reason of its geographical situation. It is cool in summer, yet the winters, shorn of their harshness by rea-

REEM'S CREEK FALLS

HOTEL AND FOUNTAIN AT ROUND KNOB.

son of its southern latitude, induce almost daily out-of-door exercise, in the way of shooting, riding, driving, or short mountain excursions on foot. Moderate altitude, dry and ozoniferous atmosphere, bright sunshine and beautiful scenic environment are the important factors of the region.

TEMPERATURE.

"Observation extending through a period of eight years shows as follows:

"Mean temperature of Spring, 53-49.
"   "   " Summer, 70-72.
"   "   " Autumn, 53-48.
"   "   " Winter, 38-87.
"   "   for the year, 54-14."

"During a period of eight years the mercury but twice rose above 88 degrees, and but three times fell below 3 degrees." "The diurnal ranges of the thermometer are very small when compared with the high regions of the west," the mean daily range being twice as great at Colorado Springs as at Asheville.

"Dr. Herman Canfield, who has a handsome private institution for the treatment of chronic diseases near Bristol. R. I. spent some days here in January, 1886, casting about for a locality for cases needing special climatic influences. In a paper upon 'Some Health Resorts of the South,' the Doctor says of Asheville, 'We have nothing like it east of the Rocky Mountains, and the resulting climate resembles closely that of the Parks of Colorado.' And speaking of the PERCEPTION of heat and cold being a guide to climate, even more reliable than meteorological record, continues, 'I traveled in the open air most of the time (January) without an overcoat. * * * I did not feel the cold with the mercury at 32 degrees, in the rain, as I did at Aiken or Florida at 50 degrees with the sun shining."

Humidity.

"The mean relative humidity for the year at Asheville from observations of four years, 1876-1879, was 70.32 per cent., while the record at Davos, Switzerland, for 1876, according to Dr. Julius Hahn, was 75.05 per cent. Colorado Springs is dryer and would show a considerably lower relative humidity.

"Dr. Denison's Climatic Maps accentuate the fact that this region is the dryest in our eastern country. The mean relative humidity at Asheville for the winter from observations of thirteen years, was 68 per cent., while that of Aiken, S. C., for two years only, for the winter was 63.64 per cent. No data at hand for the mean relative humidity for the year at Aiken.

Wind.

"I have no means at hand to obtain data in regard to the prevailing winds. There is considerable air movement which is not an advantage to any resort, but there is less wind than in Colorado or any mountain resort in America.

BAILEY'S BEND.

Atmospheric Pressure.

" The mercurial barometer registers usually in fair weather at Dr. Douglas's office 27.55 inches. In altitude which is suggested by the diminished density of the atmosphere as shown by the barometer standing at 27.55 instead of about 30 at sea level, the plateau seems the golden mean, not high enough to disturb the great organ of the circulation, the heart, or the digestive system, yet sufficiently so to reap many of the benefits of altitude.

Rainfall.

" The average annual rainfall is 40 inches, well distributed throughout the year, thus favoring agriculture and not subjecting the section to seasons of alternate rain and drought. The snow record for the season is that two inches fell on the 30th October last, since which time up to the present writing (February), the ground has not once been covered.

Sunshine and Cloudiness.

" The average number of sunny days (fair and clear days) from observations of two years (Dr. Gleitsmann's Tables) was 259 against 277 at Colorado Springs, the sunniest place in America; not a bad showing, certainly. It is interesting to note the fact that there is hardly a day in the year when the sun is obscured throughout the entire length of the day. The atmosphere being dry and somewhat attenuated offers

little resistance to the solar rays which are peculiarly genial.
"Dr. Gleitsmann, to whom we are indebted for the most
reliable data on the climate of Asheville, writes: 'The temperature in winter (at Asheville) rises during mid-day, with
few exceptions, to 50 degrees or over, and in sheltered places
with southern exposure, where patients congregate, to 70 or
80 in the sun.
"'The greater number of days in winter have clear bright
sunshine, and insolation being notoriously more powerful in
the highlands than in the lowlands makes out-of-door life
all the more pleasant. The beauty of these bright, cloudless days, and their bracing and tonic influence on invalids,
can only be realized by actual experience.' My own personal observation corroborates the above figures and
remarks.

The Merits of the Climate.

"In regard to the merits of the climate, or the climato-therapy of the plateau, let us briefly sum up its advantages
without bestowing indiscreet or overzealous praise. It is
pre-eminently a suitable one for the early stages of pulmonary phthisis, especially for such subjects as can and will
get out in the air, and are determined to take benefit of the
dry, tonic, invigorating, bracing qualities thereof — and
keep good hours. Conditions which seem to favor germ
propagation and prolong the species of the genus Bacterium
do not exist here.

"Wounds heal kindly and operative procedures of the
gravest character are rarely followed by septic infection.

"The mortality from pulmonary phthisis is not large in
any part of North Carolina, being, according to the Mortal-

THE SLUICE

ity Tables of the Tenth Census (1880), 13.4 for every 10,000 of population throughout the State. But it is interesting to note that the mountain counties show a mortality of only 10.6 in every 10,000 of population, as against 16.1 for every 10,000 of population of all the other counties of the State, in the aggregate; or in other words, in a State where pulmonary phthisis does not figure prominently in the mortality tables the death rate is still fifty per cent. less in the mountain section than in the other lower-lying portions of the State.

"Drs. Avery Segur and T. Mortimer Lloyd, of Brooklyn, made a visit to the plateau in Sept. 1886, afterward publishing in the New York *Medical Journal* of April 9, 1887, a very interesting article under the caption ' Some Evidence Relating to Asheville and the Mountains of North Carolina in the Climatic Treatment of Phthisis.'

"These gentlemen were so well pleased, and so impressed by the apparent climatic advantages of the plateau in the treatment of phthisis, that they instituted a clinical inquiry into its merits ' by addressing a circular letter and questions to nearly three hundred prominent physicians in the large cities,' many of whom had patients here. I can hardly do better than quote from the ' summary of replies ' as given in this excellent paper, viz.: ' The general opinion is that spring (when mud is gone), summer and autumn months are the most favorable seasons, and that January and February are the most unfavorable months. It is generally agreed that prolonged residence is beneficial. Many recoveries are reported. Dr. Gleitsmann gives a striking report of sixty-four cases decidedly improved of eighty-six cases of incipient phthisis. The answers indicate the lasting benefits of an Asheville residence. As would be anticipated the improvement has been chiefly in the early stages, but some striking benefits were experienced in unpromising cases. * * * All the replies indicate that sleep is favored by this climate. * * * No malaria reported and the advantages of this region for its treatment indicated.

"Among other conditions indicating the advisability of a sojourn in this region may be mentioned, asthma, hay fever, convalescence from malarial and other fevers (there are no lakes or swamps, and malaria is unknown), nervous prostration and exhaustion from over-work or long-continued summer heat; as also chronic congestions of the internal organs, by reason of diminished atmospheric density causing a determination of blood to the surface, hence the great benefit of altitude in incipient phthisis. Nervous energy and muscular vigor are usually increased, and the nutrition of the body and the condition of the blood improved by a sojourn at moderate elevation; above 6,000 feet the appetite for food is diminished and the digestive organs frequently disordered, whereas a medium altitude usually increases the desire for food and quickens digestion. By reason of its medium altitude contra-indications to a residence upon the plateau are few, though organic disease of the heart where the circulation is much disturbed must not be lost sight of. Of course those who are in advanced phthisis and are too feeble to breathe the out-of-door air, and take some sort of out-of-door exercise, are better off at home with their friends, surrounded by comforts that cannot be supplied elsewhere."

LOVER'S LEAP.

The Brave's Farewell.

Sad I leave thee, Swannanoa,
   All my sires have loved thee well,
Ere the presence of the pa'e-face
   Threw o'er us its deadly spell.

Well and wildly have we loved thee,
   By thy shores we laid our braves,
Where the singing of thy waters,
   Makes sad music o'er their graves.

Swannanoa — peaceful river —
   By thy name I called my bride
E'en the pale-face lost his terrors,
   When she wandered by my side.

Here I buried her, my darling,
   Maiden of the dusky brow,
O'er these vales no more we'll wander
   Sheathed the arrow, — rent the bow.

Could you speak, O Swannanoa,
   Sad the story you would tell
Of the braves in feathered helmet
   Held enchanted by your spell;

Of the songs that they have sung thee
  Tossing in their light canoe,—
Of dark faces whose reflections
  You have mirrored clear and true.

Do you miss your dusky children?
  Do you listen for their song?
Hasten on, sweet Swannanoa,
  To the "dead past" these belong.

Some in other lands are roaming,
  No abiding place have we,—
But, though fugitives we wander
  We will still remember thee.

And we know that the Great Spirit
  Sees our wrongs and counts our graves.
He alone it is, who knoweth
  All who sleep beside thy waves.

When we find that long sought region
  "Happy hunting-grounds of Heaven,"
Then, the red man from his home-land
  By no pale-face shall be driven.

KENILWORTH INN.

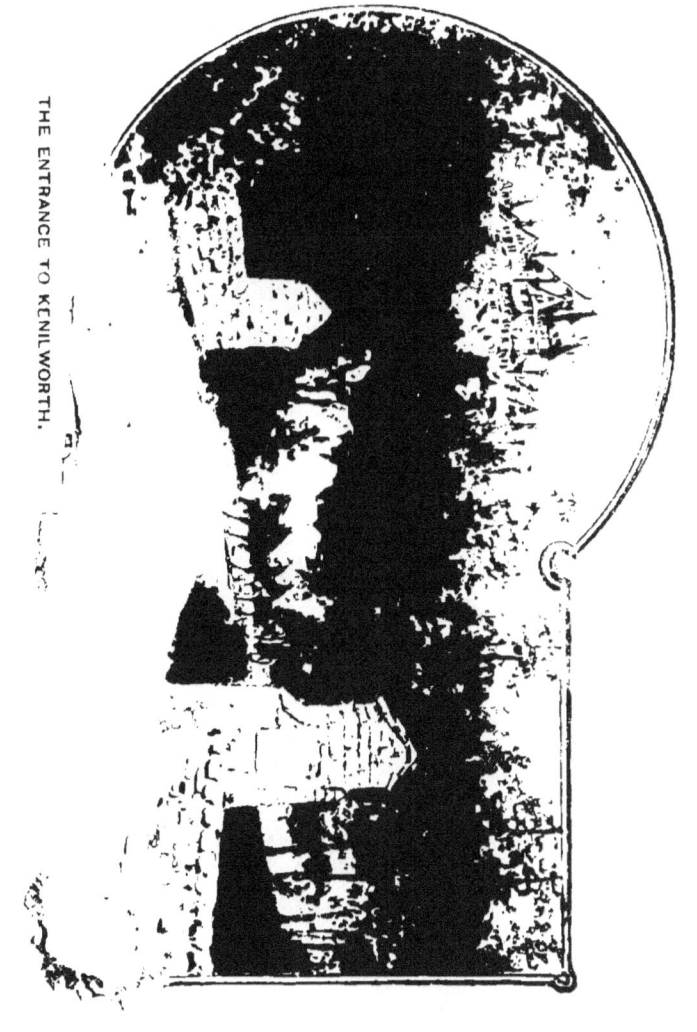

THE ENTRANCE TO KENILWORTH.

ALONG THE SWANNANOA, WITHIN KENILWORTH PARK.

HOTELS.

As to tourists and health seekers, hotel accommodations are matters of vital interest and importance; and, as Asheville is justly proud of its achievements in this direction, I shall describe quite fully the attractions offered by the leading hotels here.

AN ENGLISHMAN, a lover of nature, sought the loveliest spot in this beautiful country in which to build a home. In bidding adieu to his manor, as a memento, he plucked two twigs of ivy from Kenilworth Castle, which were carefully planted by his new home in the "Land of the Sky." More than eighty years have given to these little slips a marvelous growth; one eleven the other nine inches in diameter, and twenty feet in height, with a top of rare grace and beauty. The little, tender slips of ivy, planted nearly a century ago, by hands unconscious of the future, have given this delightful spot its historic name "Kenilworth Inn."

The mention of these sprigs of ivy from Kenilworth brings that magnificent ruin vividly before the mind of the writer. When I was there in August last on a perfect summer's afternoon few visitors were present. The green sward seemed almost undisturbed. How eloquently did that ivy-clad ruin speak of days and people of the past! The giant trunks of the ivy sent out the most luxuriant foliage, covering the old castle, which is a complete ruin! Not a single room remains to show its former proportions. It would look too desolate but for its crown of green, which seemed like the spirit of Love, seeking to expand and extend its mantle to conceal the defects of its dear object, and to supplant decay and ruin with life and beauty. Some young people were courageously climbing from one part to another, and now and then a bright face would peep through a dismantled window, or the sound of merry laughter resound through the decayed walls. But to me it seemed only as a dream of the past. The only objects of life which seemed to claim any adherence to the place, were some peacocks which were strutting in their lordly way over the velvety lawn, seeming in their hoarse notes to say: All beauty and grace has not departed — shall not depart — from Kenilworth.

"A park of one hundred and sixty acres immediately surrounds Kenilworth Inn, twenty acres of which is in a velvety lawn, the balance a superbly wooded tract of the most varied forest growths, containing grand old Spanish and stately white oaks, health-giving pines, delicate dogwoods, spicewood, luxuriant rhododendrons, laurel, azaleas, sweet shrubs, larkspurs, and small flora too numerous to mention. The native birds, gray squirrels, partridges, and wild rabbits are here protected, and afford unlimited entertainment. Looking out from this beautiful knoll, we have at its foot, two hundred feet below, and within Kenilworth Park, that most picturesque of mountain streams, the Swannanoa river, "Swannanoa" meaning in the Cherokee language, "The most beautiful stream." Three sets of rapids in immediate view, lend music to the scene, while a shady

MACADAM DRIVE TO KENILWORTH.

road. of twenty miles along its banks, is one of the most romantic drives of the many in this section. The breadth of view from Kenilworth Inn is remarkable. To the east is the Craggy Range of mountains, but seven miles distant, and through its dips the highest peaks of the Black Mountains are visible; Mount Mitchell, the most prominent, and at the same time the highest point of land east of the Rocky Mountains. Mr. George W. Vanderbilt's private park. containing seven thousand acres, directly adjoins the Kenilworth property on the south side, while its drives, cultivated hill-sides and forests, make up many miles of the view to the south with the mountains as a background. The western view includes the French Broad Valley, Smoky Mountains, with the famous peaks of Pisgah and the Rat. Twenty-six of the thirty-eight peaks known to be higher than Mount Washington can be seen from Kenilworth Inn.

"The approach to Kenilworth Inn from the Vanderbilt Station, called "Biltmore," is along the Swannanoa for a few hundred feet, thence through a beautiful ravine, and around the hill front. to the massive stone portecochere through which guests enter the large rotunda. Upon the first floor are the offices, newsstand, telephone and telegraph offices, emergency pharmacy, parlors, music hall, ladies' billiard room, reading and writing rooms, dining halls, and seven thousand feet of porches. All the bedroom floors are duplicates. The bedrooms are unusually large, the single rooms being about the size of double rooms in the majority of hotels. Each room has an immense closet, while there are private baths connected with seventy rooms, and a large proportion have open fire-places. It being an all-year-round resort, the fan system of heating has been introduced, the steam chambers being in the basement, and large fans force a current of pure air throughout the entire house. Each room has an entirely separate flue, and the air is changed in every room each five minutes throughout the entire twenty-four hours. The inside finish is in native hard wood. Kenilworth Inn has all of the modern conveniences, with everything for comfort, pleasure and luxury. A superior cuisine, the purest water, no back rooms, rare views from every room, electric lights, elevator, billiards, bowling, tennis, laundry and livery. Particular attention has been given to plumbing and drainage. The music will be conducted by Professor Bastert, with a select orchestra. Comfortable conveyance to the business center of Asheville, many times daily."

BATTERY PARK HOTEL.
Steele & McKissick, Managers. Open all the year.

BATTERY PARK.

IS a spot of historical interest, and notoriously popular, not alone for its beautiful views (being over 100 feet above the highest streets of the city, and commanding a stretch of country in some directions of sixty miles in extent), but as having been the location selected during the war by the Confederates as the defense to the city. Here a battery was planted, and maintained till near the close of the war. The old breastworks still remain, and are preserved as flower-beds. The view from the hotel is said by travelers to be unsurpassed in beauty in the world — the eye commanding a view covering 1000 square miles of the most beautiful mountain scenery.

Battery Park Hotel, on the twelfth day of July, 1886, made its first bow to the public, and entered the arena for its share of public favors. It has now (May) passed through six summers and five winter seasons, and its success, which was never doubted, has been so complete, and has so far exceeded the expectations of its owner that its enlargement is nearly double the original capacity.

Battery Park has a frontage of over 300 x 175 feet. It is provided with wide verandas, spacious halls, dining rooms, parlors, reception, and reading rooms; ladies' billiard room; large rotunda, with its marble tiling and old-fashioned fire-place of generous proportions; a ball-room, 105 x 50 feet — the handsomest at any resort in the United

States — with a movable stage for amateur performances; and ten-pin alley underneath, fitted up to please the most fastidious.

A new wing with thirty-five rooms has lately been added. It is heated by steam and open fire-places, and lighted wholly by electricity; an Otis hydraulic passenger and baggage elevator runs from the basement to the attic; electric bells connect all rooms with the office; a steam laundry, with all the improved machinery, for doing the work of both the guests and the house; water-closets and baths, public and private, on every floor; newsstand and telegraph office, billiard room, bowling alley, and many of the outdoor games in vogue at the present day. The house is provided with all necessary comforts for the winter as well as the summer months; in other words, it is built for doing business throughout the entire year. During the colder portion of the winter the verandas are inclosed by glass, and many of the private suites of rooms have glass bow-windows. By this arrangement invalids can enjoy a sun bath without leaving their rooms. It is an all-the-year-round house, and is kept as such.

A dark room, with abundance of running water and electric light, for use of photographers.

A first-class livery stable is run in connection with the hotel, where saddle horses, village carts, broughams, buggies, etc., may be hired at any time. Some of the drives to well-known places are beautiful in the extreme; for instance, the road leading to Bald mountain — famous to theatergoers as being the seat of the action of the popular drama "Esmeralda" — is one of the most famous in the South. It leads directly through canyon country, and is inclosed on both sides by high bluffs and seemingly indefinitely high

MT. PISGAH FROM BATTERY PARK.

rocky walls making the drive, to a stranger, one of pure enjoyment. For the accommodation of guests arriving and departing from the Battery Park Hotel. the house has arranged with the Electric Street Railway of Asheville for an elegant special car, for their exclusive use, which meets all trains. We advise guests to avail themselves of this car, as it is the quickest and by far the most comfortable means of reaching the hotel.

To insure the prompt delivery of baggage, give your checks to no one but the Battery Park Hotel porter. who is at the depot on the arrival of trains.

FRENCH ROAD FROM RICHMOND HILL.

THE HOTEL BELMONT, ASHEVILLE, N. C. (See advertisement.)
Formerly called Asheville Sulphur Springs Hotel.

OPEN ALL THE YEAR.

KARL VON RUCK, Prop'r.

THE BELMONT.

Location.

THE BELMONT is situated on a mountain plateau, in a natural grove of sixty-five acres, at an altitude of 2,500 feet. The West Asheville and Sulphur Springs Electric Railway extends from the hotel to the Union Depot, making trips every half hour, where it connects with the Asheville city line. The scenery along this road is the most picturesque and enjoyable to be found in this vicinity. From "The Belmont" the road follows the banks of the Hominy; then climbs Strawberry Hill and descends to the beautiful French Broad and winds along its banks to the junction of the two rivers, the French Broad and the Swannanoa. At this point the road crosses the French Broad over a substantial iron bridge and continues down the east bank of the river to the depot.

Building.

The Hotel Belmont is an elegant new three story brick building (the only large brick hotel in Asheville), with every modern improvement, of a capacity for 250 guests. The location offers the most magnificent scenery from every window in the house, hence there are no undesirable rooms.

Appointments.

The building is heated by steam and open fires; has an electric elevator and bells; is lighted by gas, supplied with bath rooms, hot and cold water on each floor, perfect fire escapes, Miller chemical fire engines, etc. Telephonic communication exists with the depot and city. The sleeping rooms are large, airy and well ventilated, most of them are arranged in suits, and a number with private baths. The furniture was selected with a view to elegance and comfort: the beds are unsurpassed. The ladies, the reception, the general, the billiard and hall parlors, including the drawing room are all handsomely furnished. The office, gentlemen's parlors and reading rooms are attractive. The 1,200 feet of beautifully carpeted and furnished halls are broad and well lighted and make a continuous parlor into which the guests rooms open, these combined with one-fourth mile of verandah, offer to our guests opportunities to promenade during stormy weather to their hearts content.

The plumbing was laid under the supervision and direction of a physician, and every sanitary precaution has been observed for the health of the house. The dining room is large, bright, cheerful and tastefully furnished. The table will be maintained at the highest standard, *both in service and cooking*.

The Belmont Jersey Dairy furnishes the richest milk, cream and butter. A first-class laundry is connected with the house. A well appointed livery stable is also provided.

Mineral Water.

At the Hotel Belmont, near the terminus of the West Asheville & Sulphur Springs Electric Railway, are located

CONNALLY'S FORD.

two fine sulphur springs and several iron and lithia springs which have attracted many people to Asheville for years past on account of their medicinal properties. These are the only mineral springs in the vicinity of Asheville; they are well kept up. The surrounding grounds and park are very attractive, and the springs are an objective point for the citizens as well as the visitors of Asheville.

We append an analysis of the two Springs:

Sulphur Spring.

IN ONE U. S. GALLON OF WATER.

	Grains.
Hydrogen Sulphide	1813.70
Sodium Sulphide,	.43
Sodium Chloride,	15.
Total,	1829.13

Iron Spring.

IN ONE U. S. GALLON OF WATER.

	Grains.
Acid Carbonic,	5.65
Iron Carbonate,	3.86
Calcium Bicarbonate	.74
Magnesia Bicarbonate	5.71
Calcium Sulphate,	.12
Magnesia Sulphate,	.18
Sodium Chloride,	2.46
Silica,	.61
Total,	19.33

In addition to the mineral water the house is supplied from a soft, pure, living mountain spring, some three miles distant.

The effects produced differ with the person and his previous physical condition. The tendency is to correct many forms of dyspepsia, including hepatic sluggishness, constipation, catarrhal troubles and functional diseases of the kidneys. If, by the prescribed use of mineral water, a general derangement of the digestive and assimilative organs can be made to resume their normal functions, the cause of many incipient secondary troubles may be removed which, if neglected, may prove to become serious complications.

Amusements.

Among the many sources of diversion and recreation may be mentioned a first-class orchestra in attendance during the summer and winter season. Six hundred acres of the finest hunting, reserved exclusively for the guests of the hotel, fishing (bass and trout), boating on the French Broad and Hominy, billiards and pool (parlors for both ladies and gentlemen), dancing, lawn tennis, croquet, target shooting, outdoor promenade over hill and dale, forest and field, together with driving and horseback riding.

The tourist, the pleasure or comfort-seeker, or those in search of health, will find "The Belmont" a delightfully cool mountain home in mid-summer and in winter possessing all of the comforts of the most exquisite Northern hotel, combined with advantages and attractions of the most perfect climate in America.

There is a resident physician, whose services may be had at any time.

THE OAKLAND HEIGHTS, ASHEVILLE.

OAKLAND HEIGHTS.

THE Oakland Heights Sanatorium is all its name implies: "A place where every appointment is conducive to health." It is located on a commanding eminence at the southern limit of the City of Asheville, from which a magnificent view is obtained of the surrounding mountains, and the Swannanoa, as it buries its form in the racing waters of the French Broad, while just beyond, incircled by the rivers, the stately Vanderbilt park can be seen.

It is the only house in Asheville where consumptives are not received.

It possesses all the advantages of a first-class hotel, and in addition is thoroughly equipped with modern appliances for the scientific relief and cure of all nervous and chronic diseases.

The bath departments are under the supervision of competent and skilled attendants.

The methods of treatment include all forms of baths: Turkish, Roman, Russian, Cabinet, Electro-Thermal Galvanic, Electro-Thermal Faradic, Electro-Chemical, Electricity-Galvanic, Electricity-Faradic, Massage, Sea Salt Baths, Common Salt Baths, Sprays, Salt Rub, Oil, Fomentations, Sheet Pack, etc.

We ask those who imagine it to be a place where only sick people congregate, to investigate for themselves, and they will find a cheerful home where everything is done for the comfort and pleasure of its inmates, regularity and correct living being one of its essential features.

The cuisine is unsurpassed, and particular attention is given to guests requiring a select diet.

Health-seekers receive special care, and those requiring a place in which to *rest*, free from the usual *excitement* of hotel life, or persons suffering from pressure of business and wearied by the cares and burdens of social life, will find all they desire at the "Heights."

A more beneficial method of treatment can not be found for those recuperating from the prevalent, and in many cases, disastrous " La Grippe," than that afforded at the Sanatorium.

RAVENSCROFT HIGH SCHOOL.

SCHOOLS.

ASHEVILLE offers excellent educational advantages. The public schools are under the supervision of both city and State. Great care is taken to have a Board of Trustees which honor their position. Under their wise supervision the schools have taken high rank.

Ravenscroft High School.

The Ravenscroft School for boys owes its existence to the N. C. Diocesan Conventions of 1886-'87 which undertook to supply the demand for a Diocesan School of highest order. The Bishop of N. C. said, in an address at the convention of the Diocese in 1891:—

"I was much cheered and encouraged by the increasing prosperity of Ravenscroft High school for Boys. Under the wise, able and judicious management of Mr. MacDonald, there has been a constant advance, and now the school has won for itself a very high reputation, and has secured the utmost confidence on the part of those whose sons have been enjoying its privileges. I feel quite sure that no more thorough and admirable school has ever been established in our State, and now its triumphant success seems fully assured. Parents may indeed consider it a high privilege to have their sons surrounded by influences so salutary and elevating, and where the training of mind, body and spirit are alike so constantly regarded.

The school will need no further commendation to secure all the pupils who, under our present arrangements, can possibly be accommodated."

There are now three times the number of pupils that were there three years ago, and all indications point to a continued growth and success.

Asheville Female College.

This college has elegant and comfortable buildings, surrounded by beautiful grounds. The campus contains 7 acres of well shaded lawn. A thorough and extensive course of instruction is given, including Languages, Music, Literature, History and Mathematics. In sanitary results it certainly has a wonderful record. In thirteen years they have not had one case of fatal illness. Its enrollment of pupils last year was 159.

The Bingham School.

The Bingham School is a military school of high rank. It was established in 1793.

It has a new and elegant building, splendidly and healthfully located on Bingham Heights. Maj. R. Bingham, A. M., LL.D., Superintendent; Lieut. John Little, U. S. A., Prof. Military Science and Tactics.

Of this school the U. S. A. Bureau of Education says: "Bingham school stands pre-eminent among southern schools, and ranks with the best in the Union."

ASHEVILLE FEMALE COLLEGE.

ON FRENCH BROAD NEAR HOT SPRINGS.

PLACES OF INTEREST TO VISITORS.

THE walks, drives and excursions, long and short, are too numerous to be fully described in this little volume. We append a list of those of greatest interest, with their distance from Asheville. Much has been written, and well written, about them; and, as such perfect facilities are furnished visitors by which to avail themselves of unnumbered charms lying about them, not only by guide books but by the ever ready courtesy of residents, trained guides and splendid liveries, I shall not describe them in detail, but mention a few, illustrations of some of which are contained in this souvenir.

Mt. Mitchell, Altitude 6,717 Feet -- Why so Called.

In the year 1835, Rev. Elisha Mitchell, D. D., determined, in the interest of science, to make a geological survey of this mountain, as it was generally supposed to be higher than Mt. Washington, although its superior altitude had not been proven. After prolonged and patient labor involving the climbing of the many peaks of the Black Mountains, he gave to the world as a result of his efforts, the announcement that the highest southern summit was higher than Mt. Washington.

There arose some dispute as to the reliability of this decision, so Dr. Mitchell resolved to confirm his former measurement. Thereupon for this purpose he again visited the mountain in 1857. In this effort he lost his life, but not until he had accomplished his aim. His body was found in a pool of crystal water, into which he had, by slipping, fallen. The body was conveyed to Asheville and buried there. A year later it was disinterred, and given its last resting-place upon this grand eminence which bears his name.

In filial devotion, his youngest daughter bequeathed funds to erect the beautiful monument which now marks his tomb.

The Grave of Rev. Elisha Mitchell, D. D, On Mt. Mitchell.

High, high above the scenes where mortals toil and strive,
    Far, far above high mountains still less high. —
Upon this lonely peak an honored grave we find,
    With naught above it but the azure sky.

Naught but the clouds which drift, and whirl, and break in mist,
    Can pass between that hero's sacred sod
And that blue dome which mountains seem, like faith, to pierce,
    Toward which we turn our eyes, when seeki·g God.

In solitude magnificent the hero lies;
    Over this lonely grave the storms will sweep,
The pale moon and the sun in turn keep watch and ward,
    While still Novembers frown, and Aprils weep.

Here wild flowers bloom, and nod, and fade, and bloom again,
    Distilling perfume, though but for a day;
From Love's sweet chalice they love's nectar freely drink,
    Then breathe their fragrance and themselves away.

A dirge perpetual the sighing night winds play, —
    Nor interlude will make, till angels come
With Christ, to bear the sleeper in this mountain grave
    Triumphant o'er the grave, and death, to Heaven, his home.

MT. MITCHELL. ALTITUDE 6,717 FEET.

Richmond Hill.

This is an eminence about 4 miles northwest of Asheville which commands a fine view of the French Broad and its devious windings.

Pearson's Bridge

Leaving Battery Park and driving down a pleasant slope to the French Broad, you cross this river, over this magnificent bridge, the private property of Mr. Pearson, whose beautiful residence stands on the summit near.

Connolly's Ford.

This is a most picturesque spot about two miles south of Asheville. To the west lies Mt. Pisgah, the Cold Mountains, and some of the highest peaks of the Balsams with the French Broad winding picturesquely through the valley.

Esmerelda's Cabin is simply a rock formation, resembling a cabin, upon the side of Bald Mountain. This is the scene of Mrs. Burnett's charming play, "Esmerelda."

The Old Cabin Home presents the characteristics of the home of the negro in days of the past. This is rapidly being replaced by the neat cottage, as education and prosperity do their work.

Lover's Leap overhangs Asheville Turnpike a few yards from Silver Creek. There is a pathway to the top of Lover's Leap, but Lover's Leap Mountain rises 600 feet higher still. Scenery rugged and grand in the extreme.

Mt. Pisgah.

Although this is not the Mt. Pisgah upon which Moses stood, it is a splendid point from which "to view the landscape o'er."

As this mountain is frequently visited by showers, it is quite necessary to go prepared for rain.

Reems Creek Falls.

These falls are on a bold mountain stream which flows into the French Broad river.

A view of them well repays the tourist for the effort to see them. The road leading to them is one of great beauty.

Cæsar's Head.

This is the name of a delightful summer resort about 45 miles from Asheville. It consists of a bold rocky spur of the Blue Ridge Mountains from which is obtained a view of unsurpassed extent and beauty.

Cæsar's Head Hotel offers accommodations for about two hundred guests.

The owner has a part of the estate under cultivation but has wisely reserved a hundred acres of native forest containing a great variety of trees. There is also a mineral spring there which is regarded of great value.

The origin of its name is obscure. By some it is said that it was so named from a supposed likeness to the human face. Others tell us that a former owner had a dog named Cæsar, and from the resemblance of the rock in profile to the head of a dog it received its name.

PEARSON'S BRIDGE.

CÆSAR'S HEAD.

Round Knob Hotel and Fountain.

This most charming place is located about 20 miles east of Asheville. It is nestled among the Blue Ridge Mountains.

The railroad engineering necessary to overcome the steep grade in ascending the Blue Ridge, is most interesting. It is very circuitous, passing over a distance of $4\frac{1}{2}$ miles; nine times the distance covered by the pedestrian. An excellent hotel is that of "Round Knob"—from which parties can take various excursions of deep interest.

Paint Rock.

A grand and massive granite rock, on which are seen indelible hieroglyphics, said to have been painted by the Indians, which have never been deciphered. This rock lies across the line dividing Tennessee and South Carolina. It is near Hot Springs and no tourist can afford to fail to visit this region, which needs a book for itself to do it justice.

Chimney Rocks are in vicinity of Paint Rock. They tower 300 feet above the French Broad, their summits being inaccessible to human feet.

BLONDIN DONKEY

Places of Interest in and Around and Distances From Asheville.

NAME.	MILES.
Beaumont (altitude nearly 2,800 feet)	in town.
Top Town Mountain	1
Fernihurst (Connally's View)	2
Tahkeeostee Farm	3
Richmond Hill (Pearson's View)	4
Gouche's Peak (Duffield's View)	5
Elk Mountain	5
Tennant's View	5
Strawberry Hill (Clark's Farm)	4
French Broad River, nearest point one mile, drives of	1 to 50
Swannanoa River, nearest point two miles, drives of	1 to 10
Reems Creek Falls	10
Graggy Mountain, to foot 14, to top (altitude 6000 feet)	18
Mt. Mitchell, to foot 18, to top (altitude 6717 feet)	28
Hickory Nut Falls	22
Bald Mountain (of volcanic notoriety)	25
Cave of the Winds, Pools, Chimney Rock, etc	25
Pisgah Mountain (altitude 5757 feet)	20
Cæsar's Head	45
Swannanoa Gap	18
Roan Mountain (altitude 6306 feet)	72
Hendersonville	21
Buck Forest	35
Paint Rock	44
Hotel and Fountain at Round Knob	20
Swilzerland Dairy Dreve via Smith Mountain	

Time Table

OF TRAINS LEAVING ALL LARGE CITIES — NORTH AND SOUTH, EAST AND WEST.

LEAVE	Boston,............	9.00 A. M	
"	New York,.....	4.30 P. M.	ARRIVE
"	Philadelphia,........	6.57.. ...	Asheville
"	Baltimore,......	9.42......	1.31 P. M.
"	Washington,.......	11.00......	next day.
"	Richmond,.......	2.30 A. M.	
LEAVE	Chicago,.......	8.30 A. M	
"	St. Louis........	7.50......	
"	Cincinnati,.......	4.03 P. M.	
"	Louisville,..........	8.05......	
"	Detroit,...........	2.05......	
ARRIVE	Asheville,.....	1.32.....	
LEAVE	Galveston,...........	6.30 P. M.	
"	New Orleans,.......	3.30......	
"	Mobile,......	8.00......	
"	Jacksonville,.	1.15......	
"	Savannah,......	8.10......	
"	Charleston,.........	7.00 A. M.	
"	Atlanta,......	8.10.....	
ARRIVE	Asheville,......	7.00 P. M.	
LEAVE	Memphis,...........	10.45 P. M.	
"	Nashville,......	8.15......	
ARRIVE	Asheville,......	9.55......	
LEAVE	Wilmington,.........	9.00 A. M.	
ARRIVE	Asheville,.............	7.28.	

Authorities.

I wish to acknowledge gratefully my indebtedness to Samuel Westray Battle, M. D., and to the authors of "Lindsey's Guide Book to Western N. C.," and "Standard Guide to Asheville" for helps in the preparation of this Souvenir.

ADVERTISEMENTS.

CHAMBERS WEAVER
LIVERY STABLE,

15, 17 and 19 Willow St.,

Between Swannanoa Hotel and Episcopal Church.

TRUNKS. VALISES.

THE SHOE STORE
WEAVER & MYERS,

39 PATTON AVENUE,

ASHEVILLE, N. C.

RIDING LEGGINS UMBRELLAS.

JOHN CHILD,
REAL ESTATE AND LOAN BROKER.

MINERAL AND TIMBER LANDS.

LOANS SECURELY PLACED AT 8 PER CENT.

No. 1 LEGAL BLOCK.

ADVERTISEMENTS.

B. H. COSBY,

Successor to C. Cowan.

JEWELER.

NOVELTIES.   **SOUVENIRS.**

— NO. 27 —

Patton Av.,   Asheville, N. C.

WILLS BROTHERS,

ARCHITECTS,

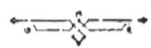

32 Patton Av., - - Asheville, N. C.

E. W. PATTON,
LIVERY, FEED AND SALE STABLE,

Cor. Water and College St.

MODEL STEAM LAUNDRY,
COSLER & WILLIS.

First-Class Work.   Prompt Delivery.

CHURCH ST.   Transient Trade a Specialty.

ONE BOTTLE OF
BUNCOMBE SARSAPARILLA

Will convince the most skeptical of its real value. By its use you can save yourself from suffering caused by the eruptions and ulcerous sores through which the system strives to rid itself of corruptions. It purifies the blood, giving it renewed vitality and force. Being an alterative it changes the action of the system, imparting fresh strength and vigorous health. The concentrated power and curative virtues of Buncombe Sarsaparilla render it the most reliable blood purifier that can be used, while it is entirely safe for patients of all ages.

The general tendency of Buncombe Sarsaparilla is laxative, but in a number of cases it is not enough so — hence we have had a good many demands for a good vegetable pill. Buncombe Liver Pills are mild, yet efficient; do not cause pain or gripe, and act upon the liver and bowels. They are especially valuable as after-dinner pills, and readily cure constipation, nausea, distress in the stomach, etc. They are purely vegetable, and we believe are the best family pills yet prepared and offer them with perfect confidence, believing that whenever used it will be with the happiest results. Try them and judge for yourself. Manufactured by

J. S. GRANT, Ph. G.,
ASHEVILLE, N. C.

Dr. Geo. O. Roberts,

SURGEON DENTIST,

57 South Main St.   Over Law's Store.

ALLEN L. MELTON,

✦ARCHITECT,✦

Office and Residence, No. 2 College Place.
Uptown Office, 24 Barnard Block, W. Ct. Sq.

Heavy Building	Full Details, Specifications
- SPECIALTY.	— AND —
P. O. BOX 671.	Estimates of Contract
Telephone No. 134.	Furnished with all Plans.

JENKS & JENKS,

REAL ESTATE and INSURANCE.

State Agents for the Detroit Safe Co.'s Fire and Burglar-Proof Safes.	Corundum, Asbestos and Mica Properties For Sale.
Agents of the Travelers' Life and Accident Insurance Co. of Hartford, Conn.	Mineral and Timber Lands a Specialty.
Fire Insurance placed in twenty of the Best Companies in the World.	Dealers in Raw Furs and Ginseng Root.

32 Patton Av., Asheville, N. C.

Rest, Comfort, Health, Pleasure.

THE OAKLAND HEIGHTS,

ASHEVILLE, NORTH CAROLINA.

A place where every appointment is conducive to health. A first-class hotel and in addition has a thoroughly equipped Sanatorium with Turkish, Roman and Russian Baths, Massage, Electricity, etc., all under the supervision of skillful physicians and attendants.

Consumptives not received.   Send for Circulars.

Asheville Female College.

ASHEVILLE, N. C.

Elegant and Comfortable Buildings.
Large and Beautiful Campus.

Thorough and Extensive Course of Instruction in Languages, Literature, History and Mathematics.

Music and Art Departments of Highest Order.

HEALTHIEST CLIMATE IN AMERICA.

No fatal case of sickness during present administration of thirteen years.

Enrollment past year, 159.   Music Class, 128.

SESSION OF 1892-93, BEGINS SEPT. 15TH, 1892

SEND FOR CATALOGUE TO   **PROF. B. E. ATKINS,**
Asheville, N. C.

BINGHAM SCHOOL,

ASHEVILLE, N. C.

ESTABLISHED IN 1793.

**Maj. R. BINGHAM, A.M., LL. D., Superintendent.
Lieut. JOHN LITTLE, United States Army, Prof. Military Science and Tactics.**

"BINGHAM SCHOOL stands PRE-EMINENT among Southern Schools for boys, and ranks with the best in the Union."—*United States Bureau of Education.*

We have carefully examined the new School Building on Bingham Heights, just without the city limits of Asheville, and take pleasure in bearing testimony as follows:

I. THE LOCATION in natural advantages leaves nothing to be desired.
II. THE BUILDINGS exceptionally fill the requirements.
III. THE SANITATION is as perfect as scientific modern plumbing can make it.
IV. THE WATER SUPPLY is abundant, the water of the purest, carefully collected from mountain springs and without a chance of contamination.
V. THE ALL-THE-YEAR-ROUND-CLIMATE OF ASHEVILLE IS WORLD-RENOWNED and with the School's exceptionally excellent EQUIPMENT AND SANITATION, gives Bingham's SPECIAL ADVANTAGES NOT ENJOYED BY ANOTHER SCHOOL IN AMERICA.

S. WESTRAY BATTLE, M. D., U. S. Navy.   JAMES A. BURROUGHS, M. D.
JOHN HEY WILLIAMS, A. M., M. D.   WM. D. HILLIARD, M. D.

ADVERTISEMENTS.

BON MARCHE
37 SOUTH MAIN ST.,

DRY GOODS,
FANCY GOODS,
LADIES' AND GENTS' FURNISHINGS.
MATERIALS FOR ARTISTIC NEEDLE-WORK.
ASHEVILLE, N. C.

BARKER'S FIRST-CLASS LADIES' AND GENTS'
OYSTER AND DINING PARLOR.
Tropical Fruits, Confectionery, Etc.
50 S. MAIN ST., · · · · · ASHEVILLE.

W. B. GWYN.   ESTABLISHED 1881.   W. W. WEST.
✠ G·W·Y·N & W·E·S·T ✠
REAL ESTATE. LOANS NEGOTIATED.
S. E. COR. COURT HOUSE SQUARE.
First-Class Town Lots and Suburban Building Lots
A SPECIALTY.
General Agents Sunset Mountain Land Company.
Refer to The National Bank of Asheville and Leading Citizens

TOURISTS and VISITORS
Will find it to their interest to call at
MORGAN'S BOOK STORE
For fine Stationery, Novels, Magazines and late issues of Bound Books.
— LARGEST STOCK AND LOWEST PRICES. —
No. 3 Public Square.   J. N. MORGAN & CO.,

L. A. FARINHOLT,
Real Estate Broker and Notary Public.
Buys and Sells Real Estate on Commission. Prompt Attention to Renting and Collecting.
☞ **PLACING LOANS ON REAL ESTATE A SPECIALTY.** ☜
No. 20 PATTON AVENUE,   ASHEVILLE, N. C.
Refers to the National Bank of Asheville, Western Carolina Bank and the Battery Park Bank.

SOUVENIRS AND BOOKLETS

Of all sorts will be gotten up for places of resort, at the mountains or by the sea-shore.

Also for railroads, real estate dealers, manufacturers, or agencies.

Special advertisements written for merchants, in prose or verse, at short notice.

Orders for "Asheville; or, The Sky-Land" promptly filled.

Any parties wishing to be represented in the advertising department of this Souvenir in future editions, will write for terms.

H. A. SAWYER,
(Author of this Souvenir,)
3402 Washington Avenue,
ST. LOUIS, MO.

THE SAWYER SUNDAY BLOCKS
— AND —
THE SAWYER SUNDAY CARDS.

BY MRS. HARRIET ADAMS SAWYER.

THE BIBLE STORY OF JOSEPH.

CONSISTING OF 48 BEAUTIFUL COLORED ILLUSTRATIONS, WHICH GIVE THE CHILDREN FACILITIES FOR BRIGHT AND HAPPY AS WELL AS PROFITABLE HOURS ON SUNDAY.

Rev. Dr. John Hall, of N. Y., after examining Mrs. Sawyer's work, writes:

I have looked over Mrs. Sawyer's Illustrations of Bible History and think them well fitted to interest and instruct children, and to give interest to Sabbath School literature.
New York, Oct. 9th, 1889.   JOHN HALL.

Rev. G. W. F. Birch, Pastor Bethany Pres Church, New York, writes thus:

For the entertainment, instruction and edification of children no instrumentality of the kind, in my opinion, excels the "Sunday Blocks" and "Sunday Cards" prepared by Mrs. Harriet A. Sawyer, of the First Presbyterian Church, St. Louis, Missouri.
The "Story of Joseph" is presented in forty-eight pictures, accompanied by appropriate rhymes, which are almost a literal paraphrase of the Bible narrative. The pictures exhibit artistic skill, scriptural study and childward aptness to teach. I am persuaded that they will not only receive the approval of Christian parents, but that they will become a household attraction.

To those in charge of Sunday Schools something interesting is shown in the "Sawyer Sunday Blocks." These tell the beautiful story of Joseph and his brethren in graphic verse, illustrated in high lithographic style. The blocks are 3 x 4 inches and number 48, packed in a neat, substantial box of polished hardwood, and the whole forms an exceptionally suitable Christmas or Easter reward of merit for deserving pupils. Mrs. Harriet Adams Sawyer of St. Louis is the author and proprietor, and the charming versification, almost a perfect paraphrase of the biblical language, bears the impress of her poetical nature and tender love for children. A small box of cards, similar in size and appearance, is also issued, which can be used in connection with the blocks. The price is purposely but nominal. — *St. Louis Republic.*

The cards are now being introduced into Sunday Schools. They are especially adapted to classes of children. There being 48 of them, the teacher distributes them in regular order, one to each pupil, each Sabbath, so that by the close of the year each child, if punctual, gets the complete set. This is an incentive to punctuality. Write for statement of prices to

Mrs. H. A. SAWYER,
3402 Washington Av., St. Louis, Mo.

CORTICELLI

IS THE *NE PLUS ULTRA* OF

KNITTING SILKS.

ITS FIBRE IS PERFECT, ITS FINISH IS BRILLIANT, AND ITS DURABILITY IS UNEXCELLED.

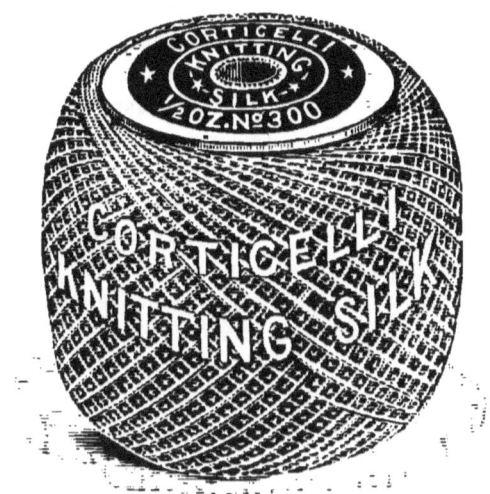

14 GOLD MEDALS.   **20 SILVER MEDALS.**

PERSIAN DYE, FAST COLORS,

For Knitting and Embroidering, for Laces and Macreme Work, it is

The Acme of Perfection.

Manufactured at the Greatest Silk Works in the World.

CORTICELLI SILK MILLS,

JOBBING SALESROOM:

415 Washington Ave.,   ST. LOUIS, MO.

C. H. SAMPSON, Agent.

☞ Send 3-2 Cent Stamps for "Home Needle Work." 70 Page Elegantly and Profusely Illustrated.

"There is no higher art than that which tends toward the improvement of human food."

HENRY WARD BEECHER.

A WORD TO CONSUMERS:

Probably there are no two items in the food catalogue which have received more discriminating attention from housekeepers and caterers than cured Hams and Breakfast Bacon. Salt is agreeably recognized as a pleasant agent in cure and an active principle in assisting digestion, but the popular demand seems to be for a sugar cured meat in which the salt flavor shall not become dominant.

Gold Band Fancy Hams and Boneless Breakfast Bacon realize fully this discriminating exaction.

By the term "*Fancy*" is simply meant that the choicest raw material has been selected and prepared by our own slow special mild cure, which develops and retains all the natural sweetness of the meat without allowing it to become too salt.

Housekeepers may always depend upon a savory morsel of Ham and a delicate rasher of Bacon if they will insist upon having from their grocer or butcher only the *Gold Band Brand.* Every piece guaranteed.

Gold Band Dried Beef is prepared upon the same basis as *Gold Band* Hams and Boneless Breakfast Bacon;—is made from Fancy Beef Rounds and dried by a process which renders it firm for chipping without eliminating all its natural moisture.

Gold Band meats may be had of the Leading Grocers all over the United States. Ladies are requested to write us for pamphlet on "How to Cook Cured Meats." If your grocer does not sell *Gold Band* meats, ask him to order a sample lot. Every piece guaranteed and cured exclusively by

THE ARMOUR PACKING CO.,

Station A.   **KANSAS CITY, MO.**

Specialists in all Meat Food Products.

McCape House.

A large, well-built, brick house, pleasantly and centrally located, with fine views on all sides.

A GENEROUS, GOOD TABLE,

NORTHERN AND SOUTHERN COOKING.

Farm Supplies from Proprietor's Plantation. House Thoroughly Heated by Steam in Winter.

TERMS Per week, from $8.00 to $10.00 for single rooms. $15.00 to $20.00 for double rooms, occupied by two persons.

Apply to **C. T. McCAPE,**

24 Grove Street, off Patton Av.

Ravenscroft High School for Boys.

ASHEVILLE, N. C.

Ronald MacDonald. B. A. (Oxford), Head Master.

Ravenscroft High School for Boys will commence its sixth year, being the fourth under Mr. MacDonald's management, in September, 1892. The school owes its existence to the North Carolina Diocesan Conventions in 1886 and 1887, which aimed to supply the general demand for a Diocesan Classical School of a high character. The number of scholars is at present more than three times as great as the Head Master found in the school when it first came into his hands in the autumn of 1889. The work done has been satisfactory, the average marks showing a steady rise.

[Extract from the address of the Bishop of North Carolina at the Convention of the Diocese, 1891.]

"I was much cheered and encouraged by the increasing prosperity of Ravenscroft High School for Boys. Under the wise, able and judicious management of Mr. MacDonald, there has been a constant advance, and now the School has won for itself a very high reputation, and has secured the utmost confidence on the part of those whose sons have been enjoying its privileges. I feel quite sure that no more thorough and admirable school has ever been established in our State, and now its triumphant success seems fully assured. Parents may indeed consider it a high privilege to have their sons surrounded by influences so salutary and elevating, and where the training of mind, body and spirit are alike so constantly regarded.

"The school will need no further commendation to secure all the pupils who, under our present arrangements, can possibly be accommodated."

Richmond & Danville Railroad.

The only Rail Line to Asheville and Hot Springs, N. C.

Through Pullman Vestibuled Sleepers from New York, Philadelphia and Washington to Asheville and Hot Springs, **Without Change,**

—VIA—

DANVILLE, GREENSBORO AND SALISBURY.

—ONLY—

25 Hours	New York	to	Asheville.
18 "	Washington	"	"
28 "	Jacksonville	"	"
10 "	Augusta	"	"
10 "	Atlanta	"	"
26 "	New Orleans	"	"

The Great Washington and Southwestern Vestibuled Limited,

Comprising the most recent Pullman Sleeping and Hotel Cars Between

WASHINGTON AND ATLANTA,

With Through Sleepers,

NEW YORK TO NEW ORLEANS,

— AND —

WASHINGTON TO MEMPHIS.

Three Trains, **ALL DAILY,** Each Way.

Between the East, South and Southwest.

W. H. GREEN,   SOL. HAAS,
General Manager,   Traffic Manager.
                 ATLANTA, GA.
JAS. L. TAYLOR,   W. A. TURK,
General Passenger Agent,   Asst. Gen. Pass. Agt.,
        Atlanta, Ga.   Charlotte, N. C.

Elevation, 2,500 Feet.   Location of U. S. Weather Bureau.

THE
HOTEL BELMONT,
ASHEVILLE, N. C.

(Formerly known as "Asheville Sulphur Springs Hotel.")

See Illustration on Page 71.

Fire-Proof, New Brick Structure of 200 Rooms, situated in a beautiful natural grove of 65 acres, with adjoining park of 600 acres, location unsurpassed for scenery; exquisite mountain views from every window of the house; therefore no undesirable rooms; nicely kept grounds; freedom from dust.

Sulphur and Iron Springs, celebrated for their medicinal properties. The Sulphur Spring, No. 2, is not so strong, but pleasant to drink; a mountain spring of perfectly pure, freestone water is conducted to the Hotel in galvanized iron pipes. Sanitary plumbing and sewerage; public and private baths. Steam heating and open fires; Otis Electric elevator: gas and electric lights, steam laundry, large rooms; light, large and elegantly furnished corridors.

The best orchestra (of seven accomplished musicians) of any resort in the South. *Brass band, large dance and concert pavilion*, lawn-tennis, bowling alley, ball grounds; well equipped new livery, fine riding horses, boating and fishing on the Hominy and French Broad Rivers. The hunting in the park is reserved for the guests of the house.

The Belmont has its own dairy farm and garden products.

The furnishings and equipment are entirely new; elegant and these as well as the *table* and *service are first-class and second to none in Asheville.* "A clean house" a specialty. The Belmont, by its location and surroundings, has many advantages not to be found elsewhere, it will afford *"the best of everything at moderate rates."*

Special Electric Street Car from Depot and City to the Hotel every 20 minutes.

For Rates and Pamphlet, address,

                                       THE MANAGER.

OPEN ALL THE YEAR.

The Largest China Store in the State.

When you visit "The Land of the Sky"

You should make it a special point to visit the

CRYSTAL PALACE.

You will be interested by many choice and chaste productions from the Oriental Potteries. Our line consists principally of French China, Cut Glass, Art Pottery, Souvenirs, Fine Lamps, Glassware, Cutlery, and house furnishings generally. We extend to all a very cordial invitation to call and see our elegant store.

THAD. W. THRASH & CO.

41 PATTON AV.,   ·   ·   ASHEVILLE, N. C.

W. A. BLAIR.   JOHN H. McDOWELL.

BLAIR & McDOWELL,

FURNITURE DEALERS

— AND —

UNDERTAKERS,

45 PATTON AV.,   ASHEVILLE, N. C.

www.ingramcontent.com/pod-product-compliance
Lightning Source LLC
Chambersburg PA
CBHW022144160426
43197CB00009B/1424